1

THE DOMESTIC SCENE

The Pondo have a proud military history: even the great Shaka Zulu was never able to defeat them. These Pondo homes (1) are in the rugged hills in the Mlengana ('Execution Rock') area between Umtata and Port St. Johns. Another distinctive branch of the Xhosa is the Ndlambe, of which these five cheerful girls (2) are members. The photograph was taken in 1964 on a farm in the Kei Road area of the Eastern Cape. Only the girl on the right is of marriagable age, a status indicated by her long, black-braided skirt and beadwork.

The womenfolk of all southern Africa's black peoples are adept at carrying articles of almost any shape on their heads – in this case, (3) a Bomvana woman carries a load of melons.

The Xhosa are a sociable people, and love to gather together to share a can-full or two of beer and a pipe (4). The women's pipes are much longer than those of their menfolk, and for a good reason – their impressive length ensures that ash doesn't fall on the babies on their laps or at their breasts. Moreover, the Xhosa have a deep sense of community, as do all rural black peoples, extending a helping hand to each other as a matter of course. This scene in a Xesibe home (5) typifies a lifestyle based on sharing. Most of the food is cooked in a three-legged cast-iron pot over an open fire, outside in fine weather, but otherwise on the mud-plastered floor of a family hut.

.The Xhosa are often referred to as the 'Red Blanket People', the intensity of the colour in their blankets varying from clan to clan and tribe to tribe. The dye traditionally used was red ochre, but today this is being

2

3

4

5

6

supplemented with chemical dyes. Here (6) a mother and child of the Gcaleka branch bring thatch-grass to their home in Transkei's Willowvale District. Children help with domestic duties from a very early age.

1

IN THE FIELD

Donkeys (5) and sheep are common enough possessions, but cattle take pre-eminence. They are the Xhosa family's wealth and it is the men's and boys' duty to look after them and to milk the cows (6).

Young boys are also responsible for taking the flock of sheep (1) out each morning, into fields where the grazing is best, and then in the afternoons bringing them home to the byres, where they can sleep safe from marauding jackals and stray dogs.

For their part, it is the women's task to hoe the fields, to carry out domestic duties, and to maintain the house in good repair. Here, Ngqika clanswomen (7) return home at sunset in south Transkei after a day out in the veld making grass rope, which they use to secure the thatch on the roofs of their homes.

In many rural areas, one of the most favoured 'vehicles' is still the traditional home-made sledge (3). It is made from flexible saplings woven between four strong uprights fixed into a heavy, Y-shaped tree-trunk. The sledge is extremely functional, not least of all because it can be dragged across trackless veld.

When I was travelling on a dusty road in the Bizana region of Transkei one day in 1979, this girl of the Tshangase tribe (2) came galloping across the veld on her splendid horse. She was the only Xhosa girl I have ever seen astride a horse.

Maize (4) is the staple diet of the Xhosa peoples, and is eaten in various ways. In its green stage, when it is firm, it is boiled on the cob. Dry corn is crushed into chunks in a stamping block and then boiled together with dry beans. It can also be milled in a concave stone to produce maize meal, which is cooked to make a porridge.

3

4

5

6

7

THE YOUNG ONES

The Pondo are easily identified by their long, plaited hair – often hardened with clay or soap and blackened with shoe-polish. They claim that the hair will grow long enough, if left uncut, to reach the ground when the owner is sitting. In the remote green hills of Magusheni, south-east of Kokstad, I came on this Pondo woman (1), who had sat down on the grass to feed her small child. Quite unperturbed by distances she said she was on her way to the nearest trading store – a long journey by any standards. The beaded band on her head is a symbol of her married status.

Xhosa homes are conspicuous by the number of children usually seen around them: a mother (5) holds a friend's child, while her own is tied on her back; in addition, she carries a gourd of milk on her head. Such scenes are a common enough sight in the rural areas. This woman's white clay-painted face indicates that she is nursing a baby, her modest headdress that she is a relative junior in the ranks of wives. She is of the Ndlambe lineage, living on a farm at Kei Road near King William's Town. The skirt of her younger sister, standing close by, shows that she, in turn, is a 'boy's girl' – that is, pre-marriageable. Her bead cascade is borrowed from her brother. Xhosa females always wear some form of headdress out of respect for the head of the family, or even for their boyfriends.

In summer, Xhosa youngsters spend much of their time naked and, where it is available, playing in water. These little fellows (2) were making clay oxen, which is a popular juvenile pastime in the Eastern Cape.

Their beadwork and pipe-making aside, the

1

2

3

4

5

6

7

Xhosa are not celebrated for their craftsmanship. In fact they do not even make their own household pots. But then, occasionally, a glimmer of unusual talent does emerge – for example, this clay car (4). At the time this photograph was taken a few years ago, there was a group of Pondo boys in Port St. John's who made small replicas for sale to tourists. The models were delightful, often depicting the youngsters' perceptions of holidaymakers' vehicles in amusing and minute detail – even down to golf clubs and surfboards on the roof-rack.

One Sunday afternoon, I came across these Fingo teenagers (3), in the area between Komga and Kei Mouth. They were in party mood and dress. Amongst the rural Xhosa-speaking peoples it is customary for individuals to stay within their own age and sex groups in public.

The national sport of Xhosa youths up to the time they enter a circumcision school and become men – around about their late teens – is stick-fighting (6 and 7). This game can become very robust, and cracked skulls are not uncommon.

The Kentani area of Transkei is home to these youths (8). According to Xhosa custom, their beadwork was made for them by their girlfriends.

CUSTOM AND RITUAL

'The shaven one' is the epithet given to the girl (1) seated on the left. She belongs to a branch of the Ngqika clan at Qolora in southern Transkei. According to a now-rare custom, when neighbourhood males attend circumcision school to achieve their manhood, girls of the same age group have their hair shaved off and dress in this manner (note that the reed 'collar' is, in a sense, reminiscent of the boys' skirts) for a few weeks. When the initiates emerge, the girls are formally recognized as having attained marriageable status. In contrast, the younger girl here wears the standard simple dress of her age group.

These young Bomvana girls of pre-marriageable age (4), in the Bashee River Mouth area, are performing an old 'fattening of the maize' ceremony.

Gcaleka girls (3) take part in a ritual *Ntonjane* dance for their friend, who, according to custom, is secluded in a nearby hut for a few weeks in order to restore the fertility she appears to have lost after bearing her first child. The scene took place near Idutywa, in Transkei, in 1982. The Ntonjane ritual is more usually performed before a girl marries.

The rural Xhosa are, by tradition, ancestor-worshippers. They believe in a Creator who cares for them in the greater things in life and protects them in extreme danger. The

ancestral fathers – going back 'long before we knew them' – watch over their descendants' crops, cattle and everyday life, and speak to their families in dreams. Because the ordinary person usually cannot interpret these visions, a diviner is called in as medium. Perhaps the spirits 'feel neglected because an ox has not been sacrificed to them and are asking for one'. At other times, the problem might be illness, possibly caused by witchcraft, and the diviner could decide that a goat should be offered. (Sacrifical oxen are reserved for major rites.)

In another photograph taken at the Bashee River Mouth area, a Bomvana diviner (6) conducts a diviner's induction ceremony. The elaborate dance rituals, to the accompaniment of beating drums, and the solemn parades that took place, together with the impressive collection of white beads that adorned the participants, made this perhaps the most spectacular ceremony of its kind I have ever witnessed.

Here, Bomvana women (2) strive for a peep at the diviner's induction dance being performed inside the hut. Translated, Bomvana means 'the red ones'.

Diviners are always conspicuous by their exotic regalia, and white – a symbol of purity – is often worn. This Ngqika diviner and his wife (5) were photographed in the Kentani district in the south of Transkei.

A diviner's medicines of seeds and bark (7 and 8) are laid out in the sun to mature close to his house in the Kentani region. A diviner will seldom divulge the type or source of such materials.

5

6

7

8

1

INITIATION

In Xhosa society a man does not automatically progress from childhood through adolescence to manhood and the right to marry. Far from it. In fact the traditionalists have a saying that "a boy is a dog. He is not yet united with his spirit or soul". This only happens, they believe, at the sacred rite of his circumcision. Until that time, irresponsibility on his part is therefore condoned, even expected. The conviction is not, however, shared by the Pondo who, it is thought, discontinued the practice of circumcision in the crisis period of their wars against Shaka Zulu, which were fought between 1816 and 1828.

The initiation to manhood begins when the maize crops, the staple diet, ripen, around the month of May. The married women of the neighbourhood emerge at dawn (1) on the agreed day, and begin building a grass hut for the 'eligible' boys. Meanwhile, the boys sit, shivering, in a secluded spot. The 'surgeon' arrives and, with a single stroke of his razor-sharp assegai (or knife), performs the operation, during which the boy is expected to utter not a murmur.

Once their throbbing wounds have healed in the bandages made from leaves of a wild plant, the young men begin to make excursions into the veld, to hunt birds and small game. All the while they are attended by a small boy from their home village and, at intervals, by a senior and respected man, who teaches them how to behave as adults. They learn etiquette, the laws of respect (*Hlonipha*), and how to honour their ancestral spirits. The initiation experience is a supremely important part of a Xhosa man's life, and he takes it very seriously.

At intervals, the young men stage their famous *Amakwetha* dances (2). For these, they disguise themselves in their headdresses and wear heavy skirts of palm leaves – regalia that weighs up to 25 kg. They paint their bodies with white clay, and proceed from home to home, demonstrating their dancing skills. Between times, in the cold winter weeks, they dress in sheepskin blankets (now becoming rare) or in ordinary ones (3).

At dawn one morning, at the end of the isolation period, the initiates are marched – or in some cases made to race – naked to the river by their old guide. Their little helper has to imitate everything they do. After a vigorous washdown (4), which is as much symbolic as practical, they return to their hut (5). Here, they are anointed by the guide, who places a piece of butter (or other fat) on each of their heads and smears it straight down their bodies and

3

4

5

6

7

across their shoulders – suggesting, perhaps, the sign of the Cross. They then wrap up in brand new blankets, and turn away from the hut, covering their faces. All their possessions are thrown into the hut, which is then set alight (6) so that witches cannot take possession. The men are forbidden to look back at the spectacle.

The *amakrwala,* as they are now called, are then marched in single file back to the parental home, where guests throw presents of money into their laps (8), and a feast of beer and meat is prepared by their families. After this, they go indoors to strip and smear themselves from their hair to the soles of their feet with red ochre mixed with oil. Local girls of their own age assist them in this ritual.

Each individual is then given a new, Western-style outfit of clothes, in which he will eventually go out into the world. But every day for a year thereafter he refreshes his red ochre and, because he is still 'a little, *unimportant* man', he has to walk very slowly – he may not run, for that would be considered arrogant. By dragging his stick, this man (7) further demonstrates his humility.

The practice of ceremonial initiation continues to this day in rural areas, although the prospect of loss of earnings can shorten the isolation period. However, fear of breaking the laws of the ancestors, or of being ridiculed by his fellows for being a 'boy' not qualified to marry, prompts many a young city-dweller to return home for the ritual or even to be circumcised, without the ceremony, in a hospital.

COURTSHIP AND MARRIAGE

I grew up in South Africa's Eastern Province – where the farm employees are Xhosa – and I shall always remember how, at weekends, Xhosa youths gathered in their dozens and went off, singing and dancing, across the veld. Their clear voices rang out in the night – many were excellent singers – and I would lie awake for hours, listening to them. This photograph (1) was taken on a farm in the lovely Kei Road area in the 1960s. It typifies, for me, the easy, relaxed and natural relationship between Xhosa boys and girls. They enjoy each others' company and will gather together in large groups whenever there is the opportunity. These particular girls told me that they had painted their bodies 'so as to be beautiful for the boys'.

While boys and girls congregate together at an event, they do not dance in pairs but rather with the sexes lined up opposite each other. Adult men and women, too, normally remain in separate groups. In this scene, a group of married men dance with young girls of marriageable age (2) in the Qolora area of the southern Transkei. The girls' status is depicted by their dress. Where there is movement in Xhosa society, there is always an audience: here, it is provided by the older women. The rural peoples are, of course, polygamous, and marital jealousy does not seem to occur where the parties are acting within accepted and time-honoured custom.

Xhosa tradition makes allowance for a certain amount of loveplay between 'sweethearts' (their word) – particularly in the course of weekend parties, during which they are actually permitted to spend the night together in the bush. However, proper form does demand that a

1

bride be a virgin at marriage. If she is not, her father receives less cattle for her under the *lobolo* system.

For generations the Xhosa have been referred to as the 'Red Blanket People'. The term, however, could well have been a lot broader because red – especially red-ochre – is used in a number of different ways to denote the specifics of status and custom. The manner in which this Tshangase girl from the northern Transkei **(3)** wears her wrap – exposing her breasts – immediately indicates that she is not married. The fact that her long, plaited hair has been reddened, and screens her eyes, further shows that she is engaged and paying respect to her betrothed: under the *Hlonipha* custom it would be presumptuous of her to 'look him in the eyes'. Her facial cuts were made with a razor blade, and cow dung rubbed into the wounds to ensure permanent scarring. Conversely, the ochre used by this woman **(5)** – as well as her dress – shows that she is of the literal (or actual) Xhosa tribe. (She lived in the Eastern Cape near King William's Town). The way her headdress is worn and the wrap of her blanket denote that she is newly married but has not yet had a child.

The old Xhosa custom of abducting the bride – with the permission of her father – has become diluted in many areas. Now, the rituals and procedures tend to be less aggressive, involving, among other things, the exchange of valuables. The bride-to-be's father buys a dowry **(4)** for his daughter's future parents-in-law. The goods will be carried to their destination by his clanspeople. The bridegroom, for his part, has to hand over cattle, as *lobolo*, for his wife.

3

4

5

DRESS AND REGALIA

While older Xhosa women may, because of their seniority, wear some splendid bead pieces, the average wife tends to keep hers simple, for she 'may not boast'. The major item in this set **(1)** is made of cow-tail hair. This is taken from the cow given her by her father on the occasion of her marriage, and it is considered to have magical properties, protecting her and her baby from sickness and keeping away evil influences. Ritual demands that the hairs be plucked from the tail, not cut, and, moreover, in the first light of day.

The girls of a family usually produce most of the beadwork. Apart from helping their mothers create pieces for their fathers, they make beadwork items for their brothers and boyfriends, and for their own use as well. In return, they are permitted to borrow them back on occasion, and show them off to full advantage. Sadly, the cost of beads is increasing by the year, threatening to bring this skilled craft to an end. This photograph **(2)** was taken, in 1976, at the Qolora Trading

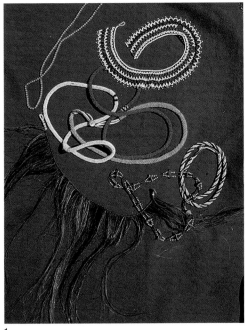

1

2

Store, which has been a major supplier of beads to the local Xhosa for decades.

In the historic highland area of Fort Donald, in the far north-eastern part of Transkei, three tribes – East Pondo, Tshangase and Xesibe – adjoin. Each group, however, maintains distinct tribal characteristics by which they can invariably be identified. These girls **(3)** belong to the Tshangase. The fabric worn by this woman of the neighbouring Xesibe tribe **(6)** lacks the brilliant red so common among her fellow Xhosa-speaking peoples, thereby identifying her tribal origin. The greyish colour favoured by her people has been achieved by beating local earth into the wet cloth, then hanging the fabric out to dry. The central piece of beadwork is unusual, and especially attractive.

The dress and regalia of the Fingo are in many respects conspicuously different from other Xhosa people. These three newly-weds **(4)** live in the Kentani district of Transkei; and this well-dressed woman **(7)** at Peddie in the Ciskei, some 300 km away. The seemingly solid white necklace is made of Agapanthus

3

4

roots, and has a small piece of 'magic' bark hanging from it by a thread. The necklace denotes that the woman is nursing a baby. When she goes out into the countryside with her child on her back, she bites off fragments of the bark and spits them to left and right to clear her path of evil influences. While the Fingo of Transkei and Ciskei are one and the same people, this branch of the Xhosa has, over the generations, tended to spread out in different directions. But wherever Fingoes live, they are notable for their mother-of-pearl buttons. Other Xhosa-speakers use these as well, but none as lavishly as the Fingo. The deep brown-red ochre dye is also distinctively associated with these people (the paler colour

5

is a fairly recent innovation). Red-ochred faces are common among brides, as is the wearing of the headdress over the eyes, which represents the payment of respect to their bridegrooms and fathers-in-law.

What is especially interesting about the Izingolweni area, at the north-eastern border of Transkei, is that many ships of old came to grief on the Indian Ocean coastline there, and inevitably there must have been a degree of inter-mixing between survivor and local resident. This lady (5) is something of an enigma. She told me she was a Pondo, and of course she was, for she lived in a Pondo neighbourhood and belonged to a Pondo family, but the facial characteristics seem to tell a deeper story.

6

7

1

2

3

The actual Xhosa *tribe* (as opposed to the Xhosa-speaking *nation*) has two major clans, namely the Gcaleka (**1** and **6**) and the Ngqika (**4** and **5**). An experienced observer is able to identify each group by the general style of dress. The girls shown here are all pre-marriageable, or to use the Xhosa term, 'boys' girls'. The Gcaleka, from Cizela near Idutywa, have their legs and forearms tightly encased in beads and their upper-arms in massed brass bangles. One of the girls (**6**) is also wearing neck beads in a fashion confined to her people. In keeping with her lowly status within the tribe, as a young girl, her head covering is very simple. One of the Ngqika girls (**4**) is from the Eastern Cape, the other from southern Transkei. Note that the females pictured on these two pages have one thing in common: all are wearing headgear as a mark of respect to their menfolk.

These Bomvana women (**2** and **3**) live in the Elliotdale district, and the orange pom-poms indicate that they were married fairly recently.

4

6

7

There is some flexibility as to when the pom-pom is removed, but it is certainly not before the first baby is born. By tradition, a tribe is identified by the colour of their women's skirts, but it is inevitable that tones will vary because individual women dye their own clothes. The white wrap shown here is new material, and is still to be dyed and then embroidered with a pattern of the woman's own design. She may, though, choose to leave it plain. The Bomvana woman in (3) is returning home from the fields, where she has gathered suitable grass for the making of her basket. Baskets like these are balanced on the head with ease, and are used to carry harvested maize, melons and other crops from the fields.

An ochre-smeared face indicates that this woman (7), too, is a young wife, but her headdress shows a degree of seniority, as does her beaded wrap. Her light-hearted attitude also has a story to tell, for a newly-wed woman must show great humility as a sign of respect to her father-in-law.

5

1

I came across this group of young Pondo ladies (1) one stormy afternoon in 1968, when I was taking photographs in a remote area far up the Umzimvubu River towards Tina bridge. They were quite unresponsive when I asked if I could take their pictures. Then a young Pondo boy, who had previously taken delight in posing for the camera, came to my rescue and, after some teasing and cajoling, they silently chose and took up their positions. I managed only one or two photographs before the storm broke and everyone scattered, and I could obtain no information about their unusual dress. My young friend, though, told me that they were indeed Pondo, of the same clan as the conventional red-blanketed ones of the area, and that the kneeling posture of the two in front was normal. He said they could maintain the posture for hours. The Pondo people, incidentally, believe that smiling (baring the teeth) indicates aggression, which may account for the girls' serious expessions

Pondo boys near Lusikisiki in 1979 (2). Their style of beadwork is common in the region. The T-shirt and collection of pens worn by the boy on the left are 'modern' touches and reveal his perception of status according to Western values.

This young man, Xhembani KaNdlambe (3), was one of the most beautifully dressed Xhosa I have ever met. His goatskin bag is common in his King William's town area, but nonetheless remarkable. The making of these bags requires great skill and patience, as the whole skin is taken from the carcass intact. Thereafter, it is cured, without removing the hair, at the river. It is then turned inside out, the ends tied off and the finished product decorated. Apart from its value as ornament, the bag is sometimes used to carry such essentials as home-grown tobacco and a pocket-knife. Xhembani was employed on a farm near Kei Road in the Eastern Cape for many years, and he proved enormously helpful to me in my research. I took this photograph of him, together with his wife, in 1979.

2

1

2

3

LEISURE TIME

The Xhosa, in common with Southern Africa's other black peoples, make their own beer. The basic ingredients are maize and sorghum, though nowadays the tribespeople tend, if they can afford it, to 'lace' the brew with a bottle or two of brandy. The women are the brewers. The maize and sorghum are placed between two wet sacks and allowed to sprout before being put in the sun to dry. The mixture is then ground, on a grinding stone, into meal (1). Thereafter, it is boiled until it becomes a thin, porridge-like substance which, when the brewer is satisfied with its consistency, is strained through a tubular, grass-woven strainer (2). This is wrung, and the liquid seeps through the sides, the sediment remaining behind. The head of the family collects this sediment, as shown here, and pours it out in the cattle byre for the family's ancestors (see also (4) overleaf), whom the Xhosa say love their beer and meat, and must never be forgotten lest their displeasure be incurred.

The Xhosa-speaking people, in general, do not make their own pottery. They use large tin cans, bought from the local trading store, in which to serve their brew. At 'beer parties', the cans are passed around separately seated groups of adult men and women. Pipes are passed around in a similar fashion at these parties (4 and 7). Pondos, however, have an ingenious alternative to the tin can. They weave a beautiful,

watertight cup from fine grass (3), though I'm told that it has the disadvantage of accumulating sediment in the weave. But here again they have an answer: the container is left around for the cockroaches to clean!

A phenomenon which is quite evident in these and many of my other photographs is the Xhosa peoples' physical closeness, one to another. This can best be understood in the context of their lifestyle. From the moment the rural black baby is born, he enjoys the comfort and security of being carried on his mother's back, skin to skin. As he grows older, he cuddles up with his brothers and sisters, who are responsible for each others' care. Xhosa homes are small and individual families live close together. Even friends are included in the tight-knit community. Mutual help is automatic, and even the smallest meal will be shared with a fellow man. Against this background, therefore, the Xhosa people lack the European person's psychological need for his 'own space', and they tend to crowd together.

Social gatherings are popular amongst the gregarious Xhosa, and the occasion of much laughter. This group (6) is on its way to a party which could last until the morning.

Given an audience, the Xhosa people will dance readily, no matter what their age (5).

4

5

6

7

1

2

3

4

RELIGION AND BELIEFS

The grave of the famed prophetess Nongqause **(2)**, who in 1856 saw a vision, in a pool of water, of old warriors; their message caused the cattle-killing disaster which I mention in my Introduction. I had long wondered what had eventually happened to Nongqause when, after I had published *The Magic World of the Xhosa*, a farmer by the name of Mr. Fick wrote to tell me of her burial place on his lands near Alexandria. It is perhaps the photograph I am most proud to include in this work.

Another to which I am especially partial is that of the old lady **(1)**. I think for two reasons: for the kindness in her face and her gentleness of demeanour and, secondly, for the splendour of her regalia, which is clearly of Victorian influence. It is possible that this style of dress dates from the Xhosa people's contact with the early British settlers. It is appropriate to mention here that, among the Xhosa, old people such as this – women as well as men – are regarded, in their lifetime, as spirits. Sacrificial offerings may actually be made to them.

The sediment of beer is placed in the cattle-byre **(4)**, so that the ancestral spirits can partake of it. They 'like to be remembered'!

Cove Rock, near East London **(3)**, is the source of many legends among the local Xhosa. It is in fact on the seaward boundary of my old family farm, 'Rockcliff'. As a young man I discussed many of the myths with a member of our staff, Llombela Mbangeli, who told me that ". . . inside this rock, below me, are great caves. It is dry in there, and that is where what we call 'The People of the Sea' live. They are those who have been drowned. They have their cattle, which they bring out at night to graze. They have dogs, too. They smear their rock walls with cow-dung as we do our huts, but they cannot go out to fetch the dung in the veld so they send their servant, the Monitor Lizard. The Lizard also claps for them when they wish to dance . . ."

The graceful Crowned crane **(5)** is a sacred and protected bird in Transkei. Hardly less tame than the family fowls, it struts around and about the Xhosa huts picking up odd grains of maize or whatever else it can find. At other times the birds can be seen out in the veld, gathered in huge flocks, like geese.

Death and burial **(6)** are associated with complex beliefs and rituals. Contamination has to be removed and, especially in the case of the head of the family, cattle offered and strict procedure followed. His spirit goes on to join the previous heads in caring for the wellbeing of the family on earth. Only in certain circumstances are the spirits of women regarded as of special importance. Note that the men of the clan lead this funeral procession, while the women follow behind.

5